MW00528442

Nature's Window

# DOLPHINS

Nature's Window

# DOLPHINS

Sheila Buff

**ANDREWS AND MCMEEL**
A UNIVERSAL PRESS SYNDICATE COMPANY
KANSAS CITY

# INTRODUCTION

Ever since the first fishermen ventured out to sea

centuries ago and found playful dolphins leaping

near their boats, these graceful marine mammals

have fascinated us. We admire their elegance and

their agility as they frolic in the sea. We

also feel a kinship with their family

structure and ability to communicate

*The common dolphin, found the world over, is one of the most abundant of dolphins. On its flank between a black back and white belly is a distinctive hourglass-shaped pattern.*

with each other. Over recent years our under-
standing has slowly broadened, and today we
know a great deal about the lives of dolphins.
Still, much about them remains deeply mysteri-
ous. Fortunately, dolphins are willing research
subjects. They often seem to be just as curious
about us as we are about them. From our
shared experiences comes new knowledge
and appreciation.

*These spotted dolphins are found in temperate and tropical oceans. Born with no spots, these dolphins develop more and more of them as they get older. The adults' prominent beaks have white on the tips.*

# THE DOLPHIN FAMILY

Dolphins are small toothed whales. They are members of the same large and varied family as the huge sperm whale (one of the largest creatures on earth) and the orca or killer whale, although dolphins are much smaller. The rare and diminutive Hector's dolphin, found in the shallow coastal waters off New Zealand, is only about five feet long, making it the world's smallest whale.

The toothed whale family has three main branches and a total of about thirty-nine species.

*These spinner dolphins have long, thin beaks, flippers that taper to a point, and over a hundred very sharp, pointed teeth. Spinner dolphins are over seven feet long and weigh more than 150 pounds.*

The small, sleek, ocean-dwelling creatures we usually imagine when we think of dolphins belong to the Delphinidae branch, from the Greek word for dolphin. Among the members of this branch are the familiar bottlenose dolphin, the spotted dolphin, and the spinner dolphin. Harbor porpoises and several other species are members of the Phocoenidae branch, from the Greek word for porpoise. What's the difference between a dolphin and a porpoise? There really isn't any—the terms are interchangeable.

*Spotted dolphins differ widely from each other in their markings, but in general their spots give them a dappled look. These dolphins have a darker, unspotted "cape" that covers their back.*

Technically speaking, however, a dolphin has conical teeth and a porpoise has spade-shaped teeth.

The five different freshwater or river dolphins belong to the branch of the dolphin family called Platanistidae, from the Greek word for flat, which refers to the long, thin, flattened jaws of these animals.

Like all whales, dolphins are air-breathing mammals that are superbly adapted to living entirely in water. They have streamlined bodies with smooth skin. Instead of forelegs, dolphins have flippers; instead of hind legs, they have powerful, fluked tails. The tail moves up and down, not side to side like a fish tail, and functions much like a powerful paddle. Most dolphins have a large, sickle-shaped dorsal fin on the back, which probably helps keep them upright in the water. Some species, including all the river dolphins, don't have one.

The most characteristic feature of a dolphin is its long jaw, or beak. Filled with as many as two hundred teeth, a dolphin's beak is well designed for grasping fish and squid, its primary foods. The curve of the beak gives

Highly social animals, dolphins such as these spotted dolphins often touch each other with their flippers and flukes or rub their bodies together. Their hairless skin is very sensitive, particularly around the eyes and blowhole. They spend most of their time in groups of a few hundred, but they sometimes gather in much larger herds that may number in the thousands.

dolphins a smiling expression. (Endearing as the smile is, it does not tell us anything about how the dolphin is feeling.) Behind the beak on the upper jaw is a bulbous area of fatty tissue, a sort of forehead, called the melon.

Most dolphins have subtle color patterns of gray and white, highlighted sometimes with black or shades of brown, but some have a striking color pattern of sharply contrasting black and white. Spots, stripes, and dappled or mottled patterns against the basic gray may act as natural camouflage for the dolphins.

Dolphins are widely distributed around the globe. Some, such as the bottlenose dolphin and the common dolphin, are found in all the world's oceans. A few species such as the Atlantic white-sided dolphin are found only in the northern oceans. Temperate and tropical species such as the dusky, spotted, and spinner dolphins are found only in warmer waters around the world. Some species, such as the harbor porpoise, prefer shallower coastal waters. The river dolphins are found in the fresh water of huge rivers such as the Amazon and Ganges.

# SWIMMING AND DIVING

To catch their fast-moving prey, dolphins must be able to swim rapidly and dive deeply. Ocean-dwelling dolphins such as the bottlenose can swim at speeds of up to fifteen miles per hour. Spotted dolphins can put on bursts of speed that reach twenty-five miles per hour. To attain its top speed, a dolphin "porpoises" by leaping out of the water repeatedly in a series of forward-moving arcs. Dolphins can also "tail walk" or hold themselves upright above the water by moving

*Dolphins are superb swimmers. Their streamlined bodies are perfectly designed for gliding almost effortlessly through the water. These spotted dolphins can even swim upside down.*

their powerful tail flukes, somewhat like a human tread-

ing water to stay afloat.

Some dolphins are especially acrobatic. The spinner

dolphin, as its name suggests, spins around in the air—

as many as four times—during a leap. Dusky dolphins

are also quite athletic, often doing head-over-tail somer-

saults. Dolphin acrobatics are usually part of the pursuit

of prey. By leaping into the air or tail walking, for exam-

ple, a dolphin can scan the surface of the ocean and look

for seabirds feeding on schools of fish near the surface.

Often dolphins seem to leap and frolic just for fun. Dolphins are often seen riding along on the bow wave of a ship at sea or leaping in and out of the wake, for no apparent reason other than sheer enjoyment. Dolphins have also been observed blowing rings of air in the water, like smokers making smoke rings, simply for their own amusement. As anyone who has ever visited an aquarium knows, dolphins seem to enjoy being around people and showing off their acrobatic skills.

Dolphins are excellent divers as well. Bottlenose

These bottlenose dolphins are "porpoising," or moving forward very quickly by leaping out of the water. Bottlenose dolphins, found in the warm areas of every ocean, are perhaps the best known of all dolphins. They are also one of the most robust, reaching lengths of nearly fifteen feet and weighing some six hundred pounds.

These dolphins generally live in small groups in coastal waters. During their annual migrations, they can often be seen traveling in large groups along the coasts of California and from North Carolina to Florida.

dolphins reach depths of three hundred feet and stay underwater for seven minutes. Dall's porpoises, found in the northern Pacific Ocean, can dive to five hundred feet.

Dolphins can stay underwater for so long because they breathe very efficiently. A dolphin's "nostrils" are its blowhole, a crescent-shaped opening on the top of its head. When the dolphin surfaces, it opens its blowhole, exhales explosively, and then inhales deeply, exchanging 80 percent of the gases in its lungs. By contrast, we exchange only about 30 percent.

*Found only in the temperate waters of the northern Pacific Ocean, the Pacific white-sided dolphin has sharply contrasting colors and a highly distinct hooked dorsal fin on its back.*

# DOLPHIN SOCIETY

Dolphins are social animals that usually live in groups. The size of the group varies considerably depending on the species. Bottlenose and spotted dolphins, for example, generally live in small groups of about ten. The groups are fluid, however, and change in size and membership for reasons that are often not clear to us.

Common dolphins and several other species live in huge herds that contain hundreds or sometimes even thousands of members.

*Dolphins' tail flukes, flat and horizontal, are made of tendons and muscles but no bones. To swim, the dolphin uses its powerful tail muscles to move the flukes up and down like a paddle.*

Research has revealed that dolphins are surprisingly long-lived. Bottlenose males live into their forties, females into their fifties. A female will have a single calf once every three years or so. When the calf is born, it swims instinctively to the surface to take its first breath.

Since the shape of a dolphin's beak makes suckling underwater impossible, the mother dolphin feeds her calf by squirting her milk into its mouth. For about two to three years, the calf stays with its mother, gradually becoming less dependent on her milk while learning to catch fish on its own. The father dolphin has no part in raising the young calf.

Although there are many tales of dolphins lifting an injured group member up to breathe, or even of helping keep a human afloat in the water, researchers aren't really sure if this is true cooperative behavior. Most of the stories, on closer examination, turn out to be exaggerations or misinterpretations. But dolphins definitely do act cooperatively in the pursuit of prey. Bottlenose dolphins, for example, act together to drive schools of

Within a herd, the dolphins tend to group together by age and sex. The females with calves (babies), such as these spotted dolphins, form one group, while juvenile males form another, and adult males yet another. When the herd is threatened, the mothers and babies move toward the center and are protected by the larger males and childless females.

fish into shallow water where they will be easy to catch.

Some dolphin species are migratory, regularly moving with the seasons to follow their prey. Off the California coast bottlenose dolphins can be seen as they migrate south every autumn and return north every spring. In the Atlantic, migrating bottlenose dolphins are easily seen as they come close to the North Carolina coastline. Harbor porpoises in the Baltic Sea and striped dolphins off the coast of Japan also migrate in predictable patterns.

*The highly social Pacific white-sided dolphins form large herds of hundreds or even a thousand; and these gregarious dolphins often are found in the company of other species such as the humpback whale.*

# Dolphin communication

One of the most fascinating aspects of dolphins and their society is their ability to communicate through sound. The noises are produced in air sacs near the dolphin's blowhole. Every dolphin has its own unique voice—a special whistling sound that identifies an individual dolphin to the others in the area. By varying its vocal signature, a dolphin can communicate information, such as the presence of a dangerous shark, to other members of the herd.

*Although these bottlenose dolphins appear to be "talking" to each other, the noise is coming not from their open mouths but from air chambers above and behind their eyes, near the blowhole.*

Unlike larger whales, whose noises travel underwater for hundreds of miles, dolphin sounds don't go very far. Dolphin groups whistle constantly to help them stay close together. They also make a wide variety of other sounds—buzzes, pops, clicks, and squeaks. We don't really know what all the noise is about, although the dolphins may be expressing emotions such as anger or excitement.

*Dolphins communicate with each other all the time, keeping each other informed of their locale and surroundings. The sounds are high-pitched whistles that are often inaudible to human ears.*

Dolphins make long strings of rapid, clicking noises that are used for echolocation—the animal version of sonar. When the click sound

waves strike an object such as a fish, they are bounced back to the dolphin. By evaluating the echoes, the dolphin can track and home in on the fish. Most researchers believe that the melon in a dolphin's head plays an important role in echolocation by aiming the clicks outward and ahead. Amazingly, a dolphin's built-in sonar is so sophisticated that it can echolocate on both near and distant targets at the same time.

When chasing fish, dolphins may make bursts of high-frequency sound too high-pitched for humans to hear. These powerful bursts of sound waves may be used to stun or even kill the fish.

Because dolphins have unusually large brains, communicate with each other, act cooperatively, and readily learn complicated tasks and tricks in captivity, at one time researchers thought they were as intelligent as humans. More recent research has shown that while dolphins are undeniably intelligent and playful, they are not really much smarter than other marine mammals, such as seals, and are less intelligent than many land mammals.

# THREATS TO DOLPHINS

In nature, dolphins have few enemies. Only sharks and orcas prey on them. Sharks are especially dangerous. In one study of bottlenose dolphins, nearly a quarter of them had scars from shark attacks. By far the biggest threat to all dolphins today is uncontrolled fishing. Dolphins often become hopelessly entangled in the huge drift nets, often several miles long, set out by fleets of fishing boats. Unable to rise to the surface to breathe, the dolphins drown.

*The increasingly rare Commerson's dolphin, found in the cold ocean waters of the subantarctic, are small and chunky with striking black and white markings. Overhunting by fishermen is a threat.*

Every year, tens of thousands of dolphins of all species die in these fishnet accidents.

Tuna fishing with nets is another major threat. In the eastern tropical waters of the Pacific Ocean, fishing boats deliberately search for dolphins, especially spotted and spinner dolphins. The reason is that in that part of the ocean herds of dolphins are often found swimming above schools of valuable yellowfin tuna. The fishing boat encircles the tuna school with a huge purse net that can be closed at the bottom. The net then pulls in the tuna—

along with the dolphins. Since the purse net came into use in the 1950s, millions of dolphins have been killed.

Although improved fishing techniques have lessened the numbers of dolphin netted, many thousands are still killed every year. Public outcry over the slaughter has led to legislation that prohibits the sale of net-caught tuna in America. Today, dolphin-safe tuna is helping to preserve the endangered populations of spinner and spotted dolphins. Not all nations have similar laws, however, and the battle to protect the dolphin continues.

Another serious global threat to dolphins is the degradation of their environment by water pollution. In southern Florida, for example, researchers found that most firstborn bottlenose calves die within their first year. It is believed that this is because chemical toxins from the environment concentrate in the mother's milk. Later calves often survive because the mother dolphin will then have fewer accumulated toxins, but the firstborn calf is usually overwhelmed by the poisons and dies.

*Bottlenose dolphins thrive in captivity when they are treated humanely. The dolphins show affection for their trainers and seem to enjoy performing for them, a trait visible to anyone at an aquarium show.*

# DOLPHINS AND HUMANS

The many species in the large and interesting dolphin family are all intelligent, social, and well adapted for their life in the water. We love to watch them as they glide easily through the water and leap gracefully through the air; we enjoy seeing captive dolphins perform tricks with such apparent pleasure. Even in the wild, they are interested in and surprisingly tolerant of us. For dolphins to remain with us and future generations, we must protect and preserve them.

*A Pacific white-sided dolphin leaps out of the water in the coastal sea of the Pacific Northwest. Dolphins thrive on the abundant fish in this stunningly beautiful and pollution-free area.*

**Photography credits**
All images provided by Ellis Nature Photography
©Brandon D. Cole: pages 2, 7, 11, 14-15, 19, 25, 26, 30-31, 37
©Konrad Wothe: pages 4, 22-23, 44
©Paul Schroeder: pages 32, 47
©Andy Caulfield: pages 8, 35
©Gerry Ellis: page 40
Front jacket: ©Brandon D. Cole
Back jacket: ©Konrad Wothe

ISBN: 0-8362-2783-2

Printed in Hong Kong

First U.S. edition
1   3   5   7   9   10   8   6   4   2

Editor: Linda Hetzer
Art director: Susi Oberhelman
Designer: Yolanda Monteza

Produced by Smallwood and Stewart, Inc., New York City